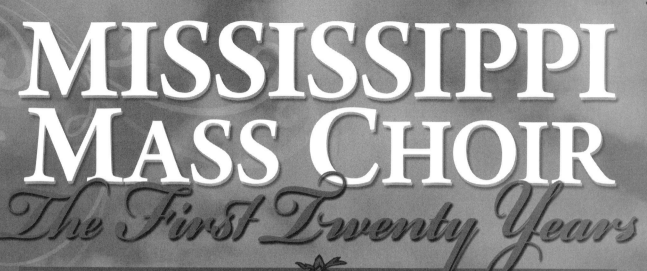

# MISSISSIPPI MASS CHOIR
## The First Twenty Years

## Shawnee Press, Inc.

*A Subsidiary of Music Sales Corporation*
**1107 17th Avenue South • Nashville, TN 37212**

Visit Shawnee Press Online at www.shawneepress.com/songbooks

# CONTENTS

# Mississippi Mass Choir
## The First Twenty Years

Some faces have changed in the Mississippi Mass Choir since its start 20 years ago, but the choir's mission remains the same.  "We are still about the business of evangelizing the world in song," says the Rev. Benjamin Cone, president of the Good Samaritan Ministries, who serves as spiritual advisor."  "The Lord put us together for that purpose and we still look to Him for guidance."

Founded by the late Frank Williams, a well-known songwriter, gospel singer and record company executive who died in 1993, the choir continues to strive for gospel excellance.  Its goal is to be more than just another choir singing God's praises.  It wants to be a ministry that leads lost souls to Christ.

The first person Williams contacted when he decided to start the Mass Choir was David Curry, an old friend and former minister of music at Liberal Trinity Church of God in Christ in Jackson.  "We had worked with him on several projects," recalls Curry, "I was really excited about it because it was something I had wanted to do.  God sent Frank my way."

The two, along with Jerry Smith, held open auditions for the choir that currently has about 150 members.  High schoolers, retirees and people in between all came to showcase their talent.  The choir's members are students, nurses, police officers, doctors, teachers, truckers and people of various professions."  The Lord hand-picked all of us," says Rev. Cone.  In October 1988, only five months after the group's first rehearsal, the choir recorded its first album and video at Thalia Mara Hall in Jackson.

The choir's debut album, "The Mississippi Mass Choir Live", remained in the No. 1 slot atop the Billboard magazine chart for 45 consecutive weeks, setting a record for a recording of any music genre.  For its popularity, the magazine gave the choir a Special Achievement Award.  Additional honors include the 1997 Stellar Awards as *Choir of the Year* and *Traditional Choir of the Year* and a Grammy nomination.  They also received a 2nd Grammy nomination of the CD "Emmanuel" in 2000.

Executive Director Jerry Mannery contends that God has blessed the choir because it has not lost its focus.  "We are all about our Father's Business," says Mannery.  We are not entertainers.  We are ministers for Christ."

Those who have seen the Mississippi Mass in concert know there is something different about this group of singers.  Their music penetrates to the soul and lifts people of all ages from their seats in fervent praise to the Almighty God.  Hands raised, tears flow, and people clap, dance and sing to the Lord. Concerts always end with a mini-sermon and alter call by Rev. Cone or a designated member of the choir's team of spiritual advisors.

 "We never want to leave without giving people an opportunity to accept the Lord," says Rev. Cone.  "That's the most important part of any service we may give."

The choir has a massive following in the United States and in recent years has gained international fans as well. It has toured Japan, Italy, Spain, Portugal, France, and Greece, becoming the first gospel group to perform at the Theater of Herodes Atticus, at the ancient Acropolis in Athens. The choir was unexpectedly invited to sing for Pope John Paul II at his summer residence in Castel Gandolfo, after performing at the famed Umbria Jazz Gospel & Soul Easter Festival in Terni, Italy.

The choir still has 50 percent of its original members, the majority of the original musicians, ministers of music, choir director and the initial executive board.  "God is still with us," says Rev. Cone. "He is the author and finisher of our mission.  We count it a high and holy privilege to represent Him and the state of Mississippi wherever we go."

*— Jerry Mannery, Executive Director, MMC*

# God Gets the Glory

*Piano Score by*
**DON THIGPEN**

*Words and Music by*
**DAVID CURRY**
*and* **STEVE HARRISON**

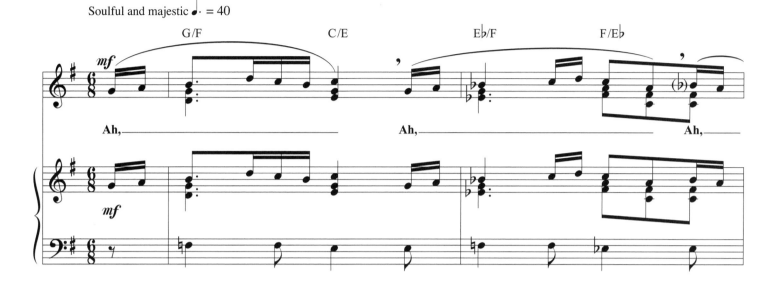

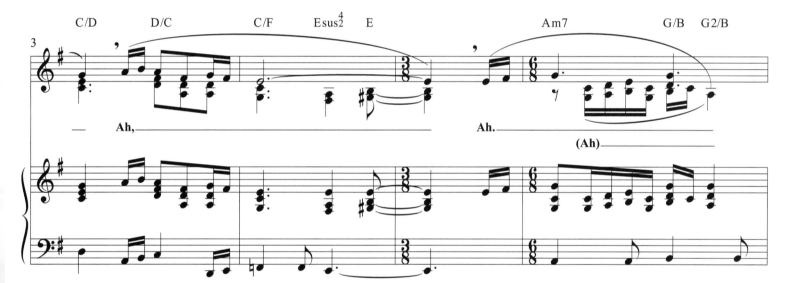

# It Wasn't The Nails

Piano Score by
**DON T. THIGPEN**

*Words and Music by*
**JERRY MANNERY**
*and* **MILTON BIGGHAM**

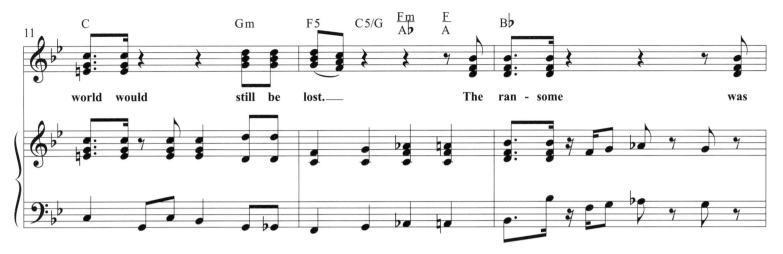

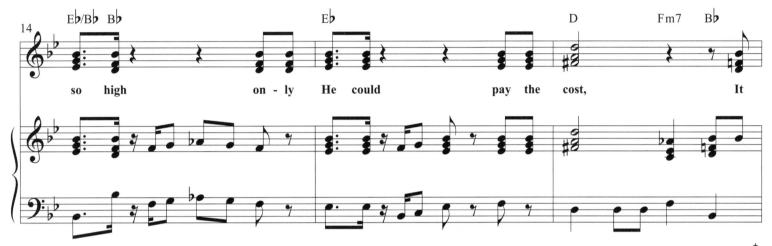

*Last time to Coda* ⊕

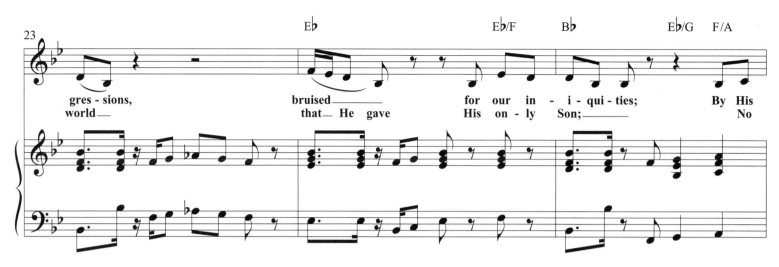

# Amazing Love

*Piano Score by*
**DON T. THIGPEN**

*Words and Music by*
**JERRY MANNERY**
*and* **DAVID R. CURRY**

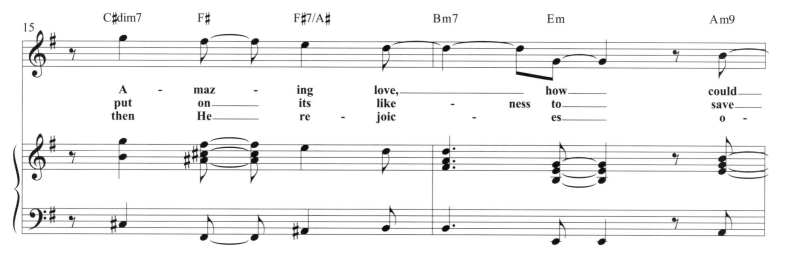

no - bod - y but You.___ This is___ some - thing, Lord,___

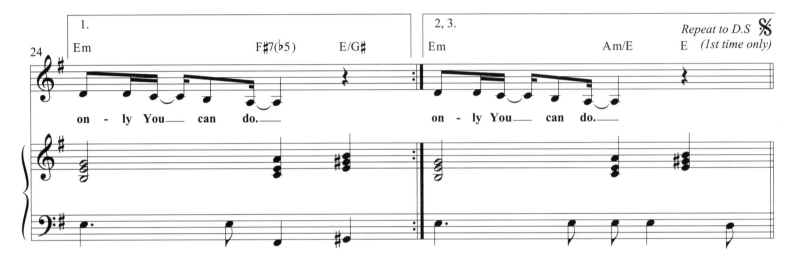

on - ly You___ can do.___ on - ly You___ can do.___

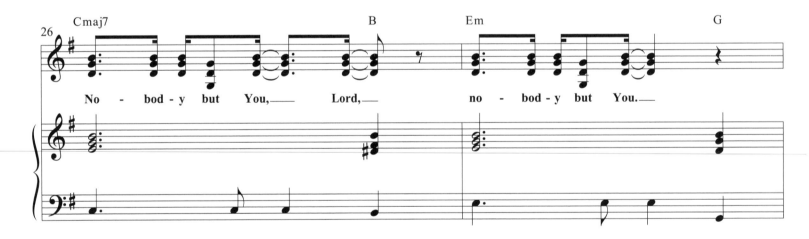

No - bod - y but You,___ Lord,___ no - bod - y but You.___

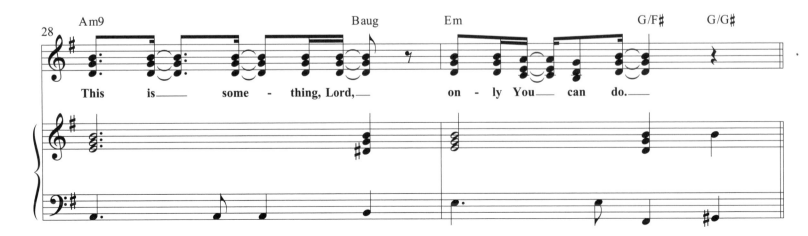

This is___ some - thing, Lord,___ on - ly You___ can do.___

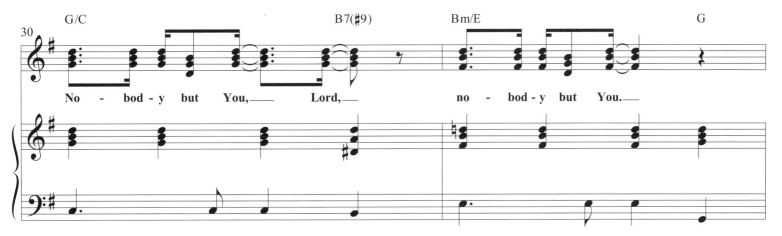

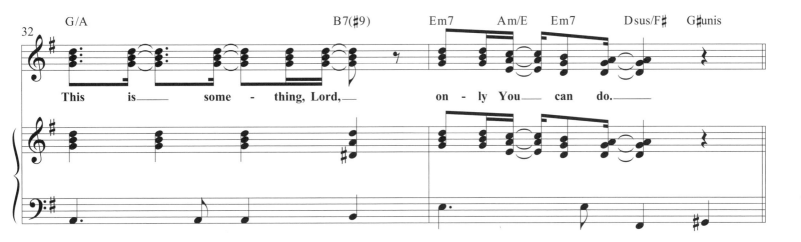

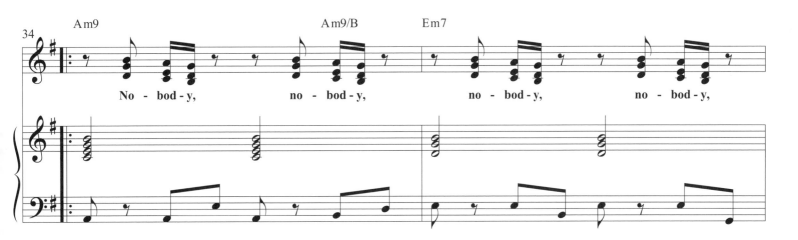

*Repeat as desired*

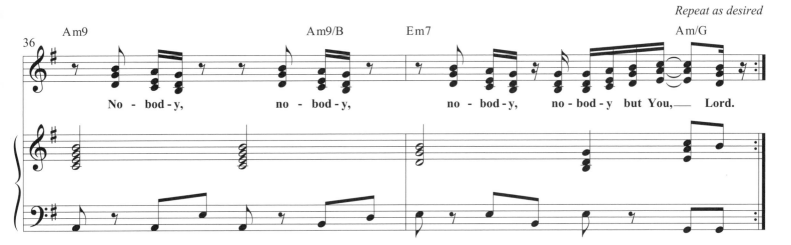

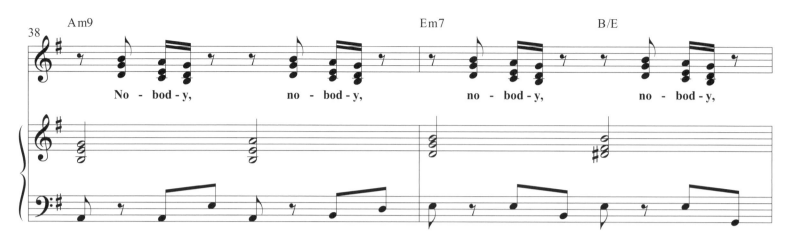

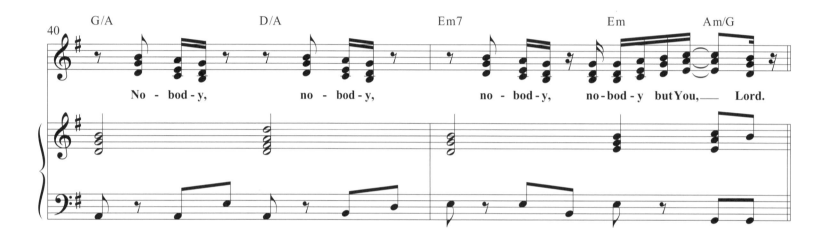

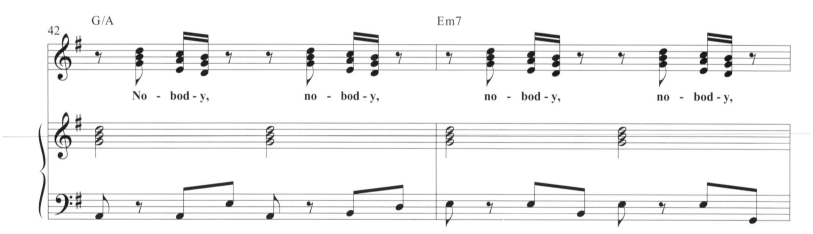

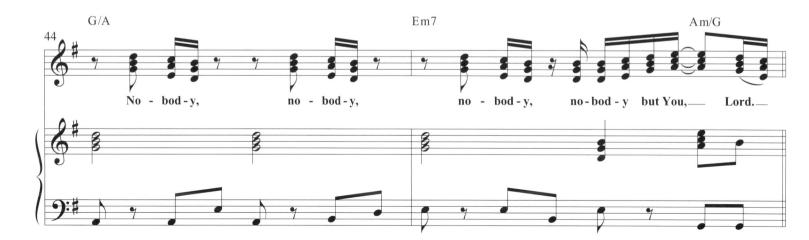

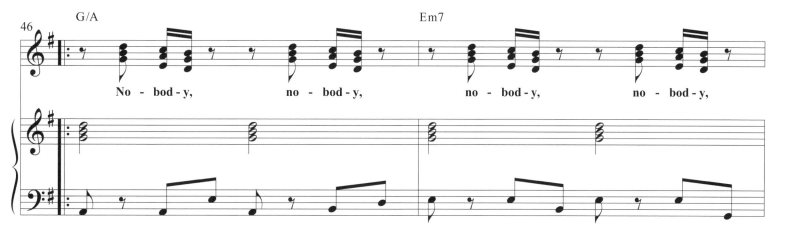

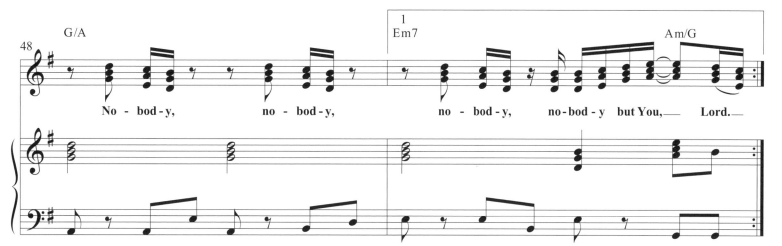

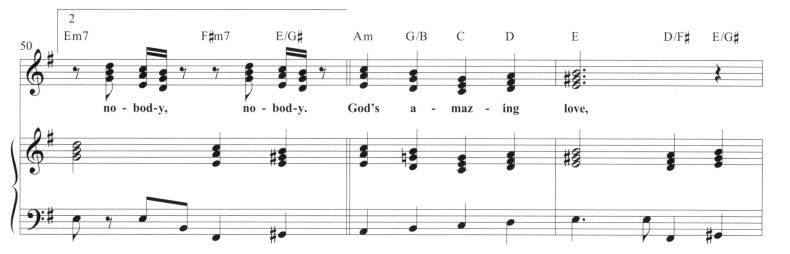

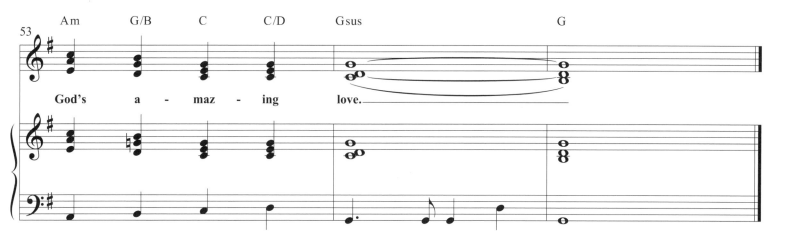

# I Need Thee

*Piano Score by*
**DON THIGPEN**

*Arranged by*
**JERRY CALVIN SMITH**

*Suggestions for Vamp at end of Song (measure 49):*

1. Soloist ad libs 4 times (16 bars)
2. Altos and Soloist 2 times (8 bars)
3. Tenors, Altos, and Soloist 2 times
4. The entire Choir and Soloist carry song out

The Soloist ad libs also whenever the Choir is singing.

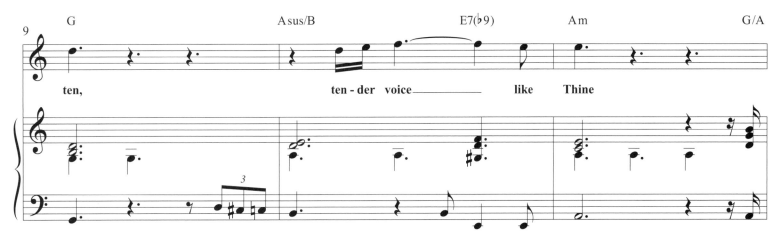

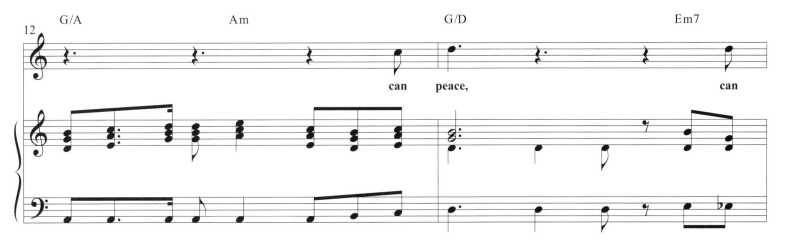

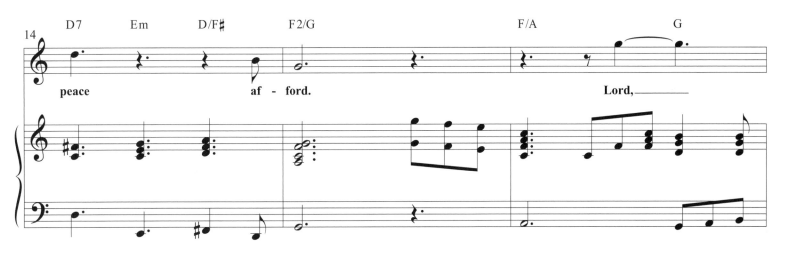

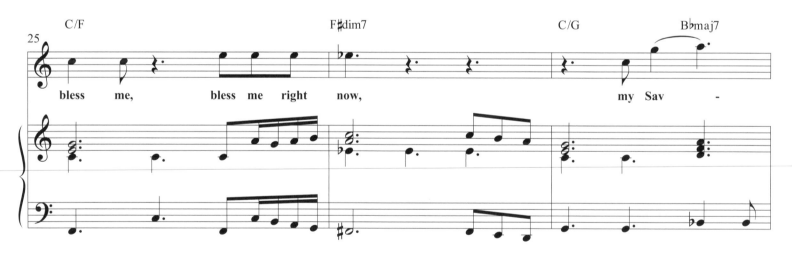

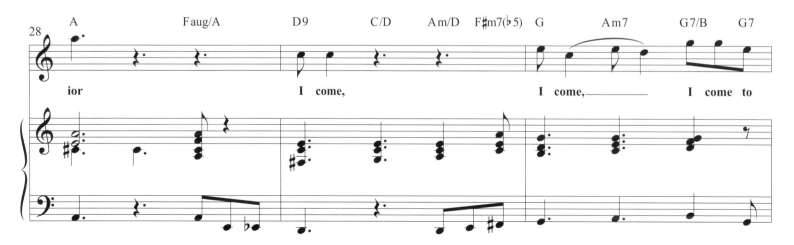

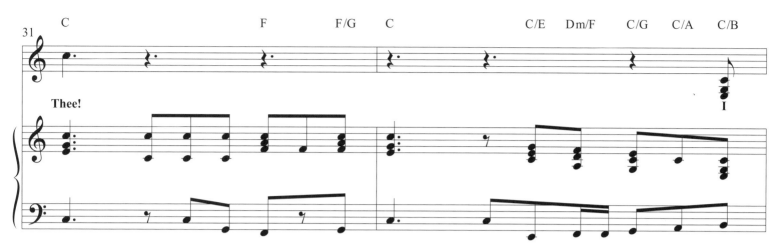

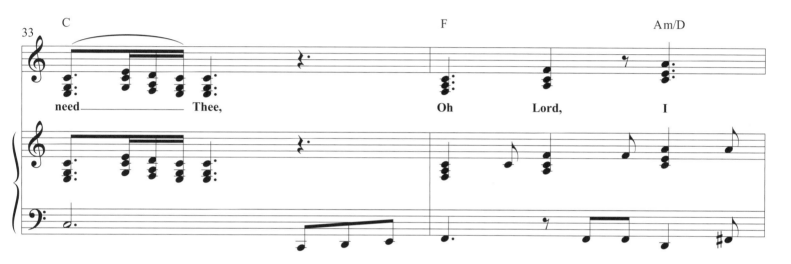

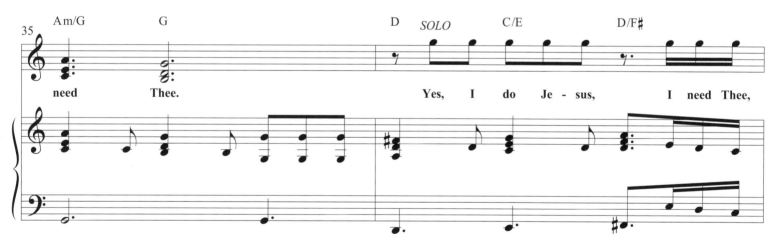

# This Morning When I Rose

*Piano Score by*
**ANDREW J. LEWIS**

*Words and Music by*
**H. L. PARKER** *and* **CARLTON REESE**

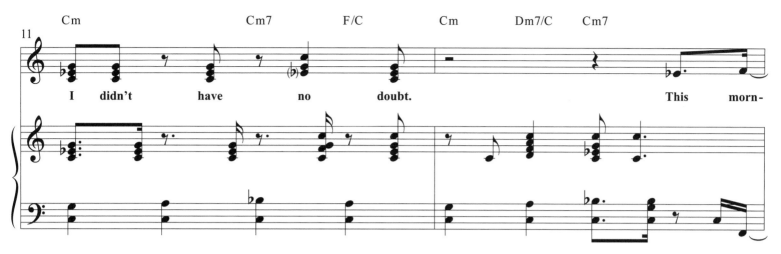

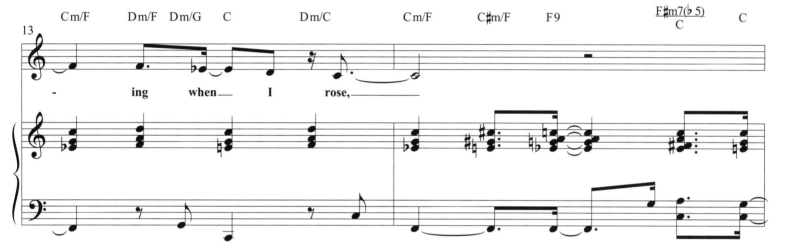

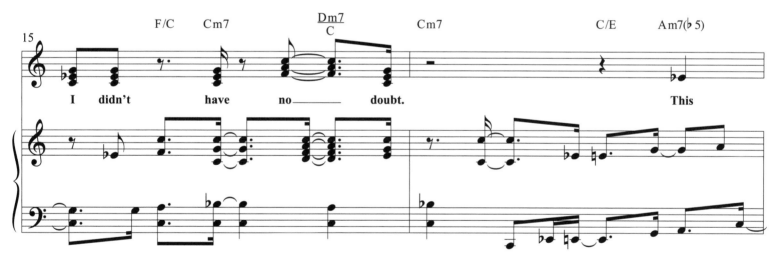

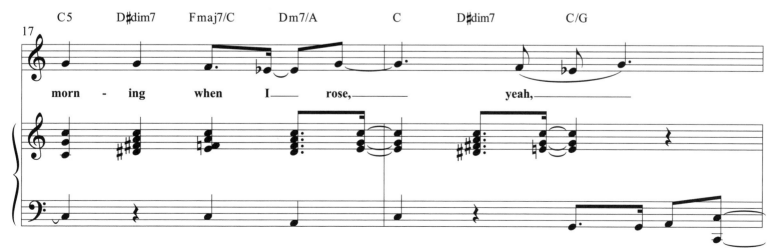

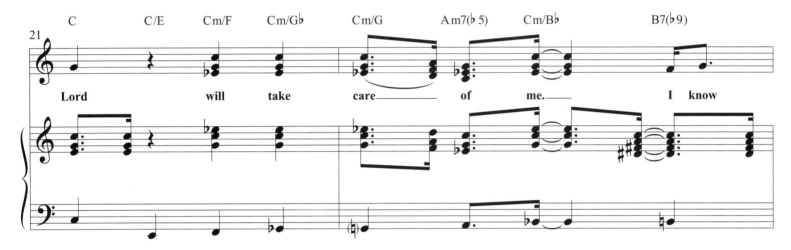

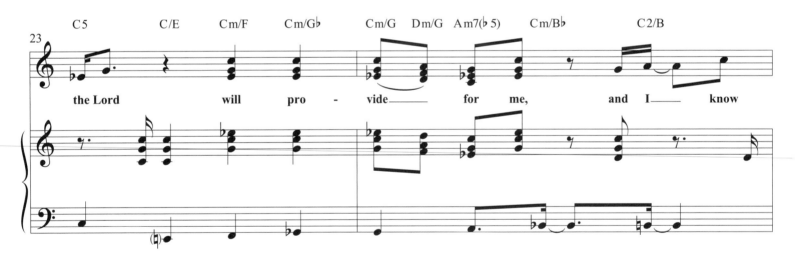

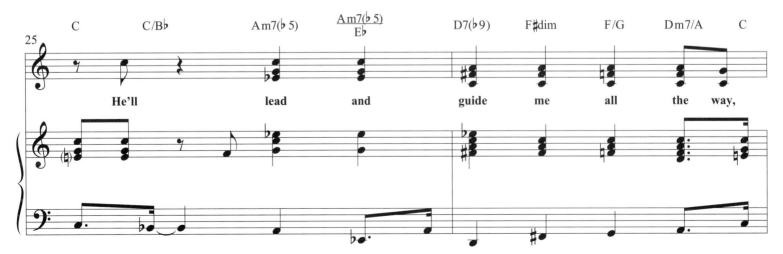

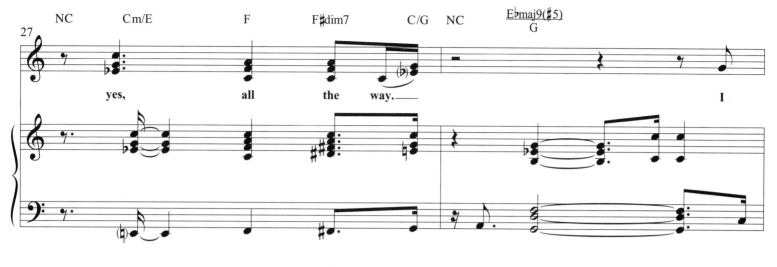

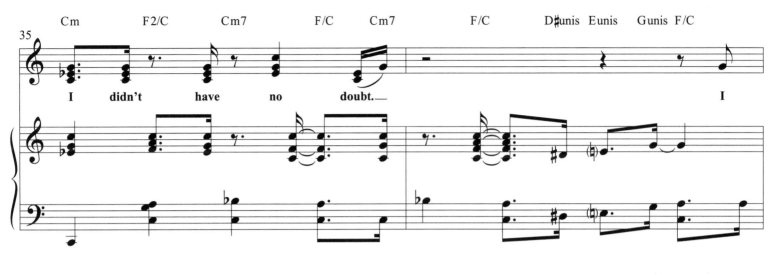

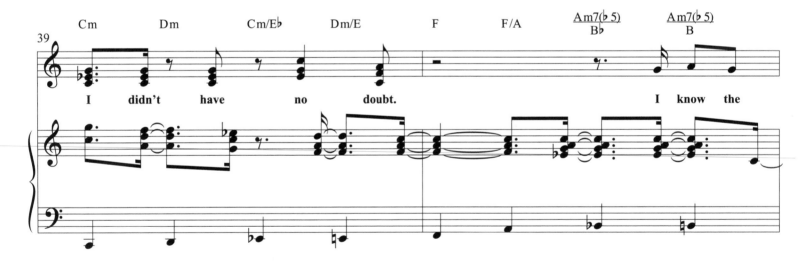

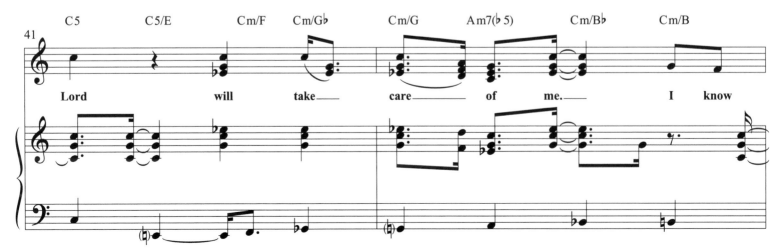

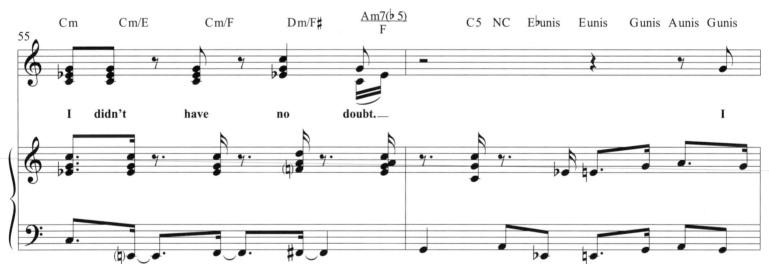

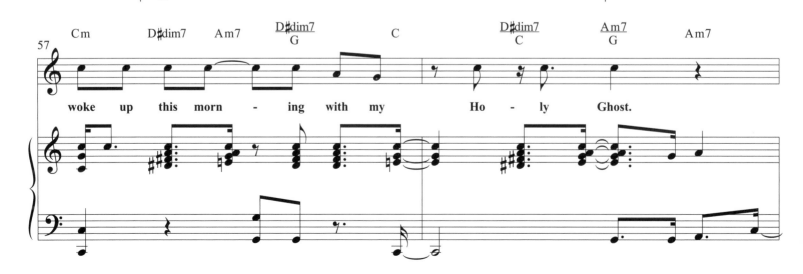

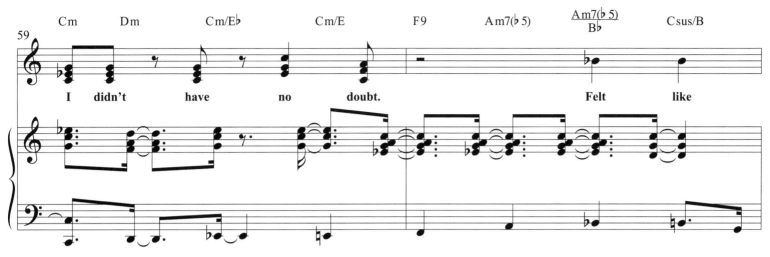

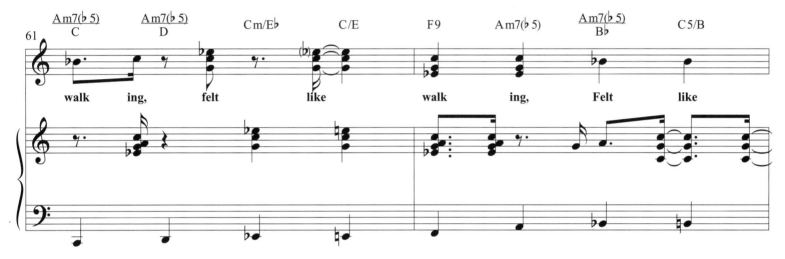

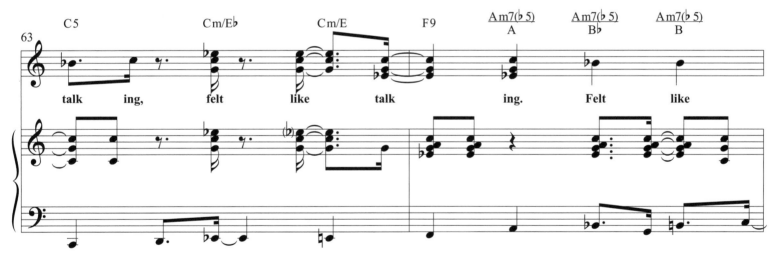

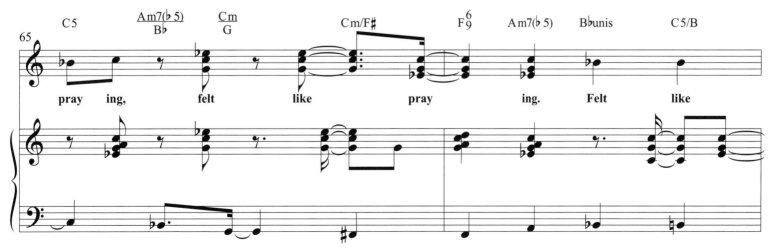

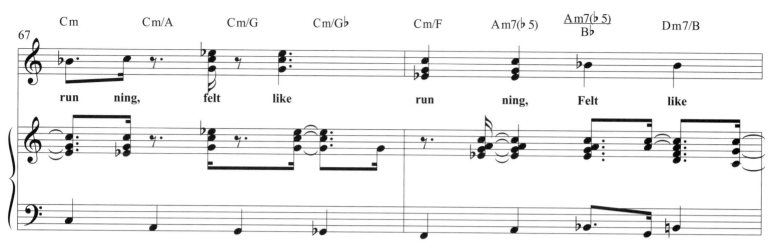

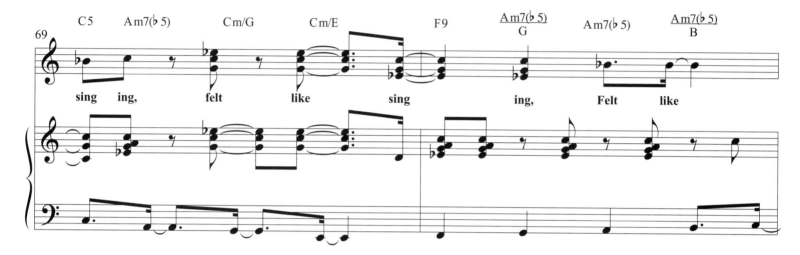

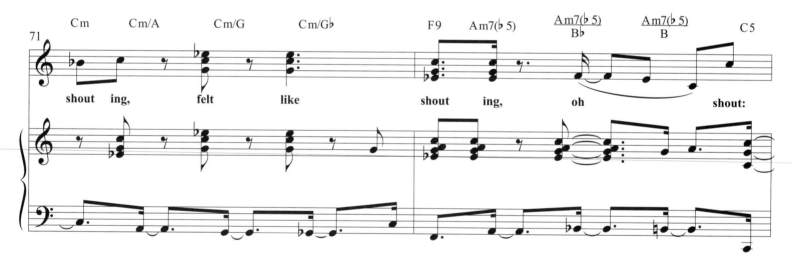

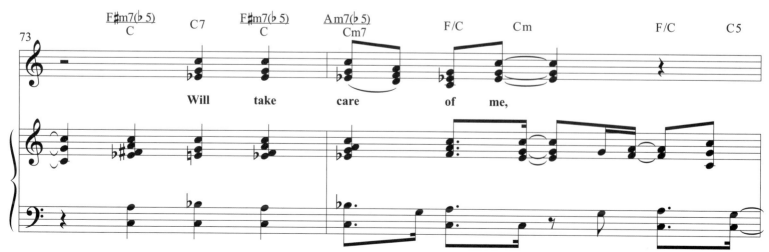

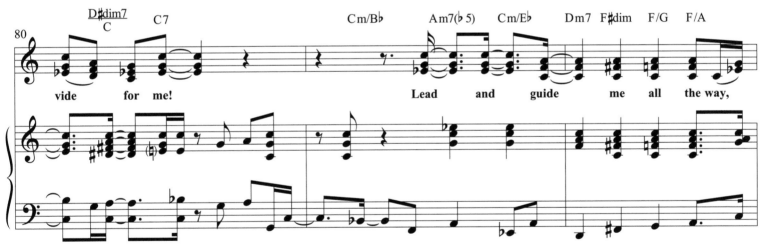

# God Has a Chosen People

*Piano Score by*
**ANDREW J. LEWIS**

*Words and Music by*
**JERRY MANNERY**
*and* **DAVID R. CURRY**

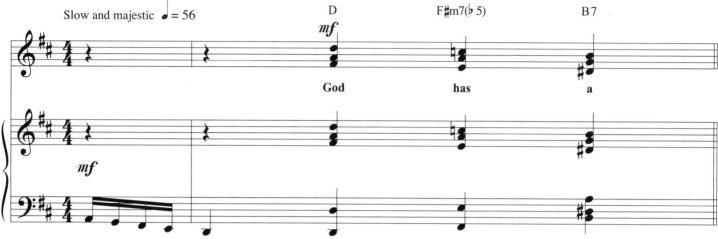

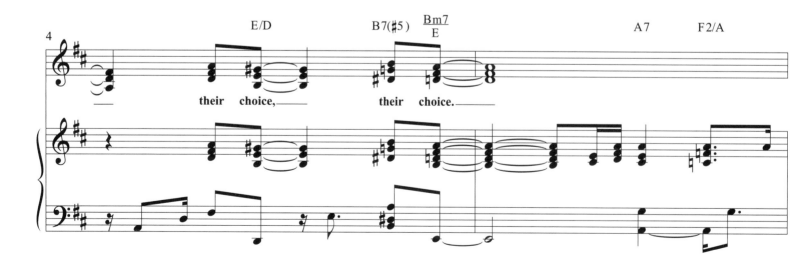

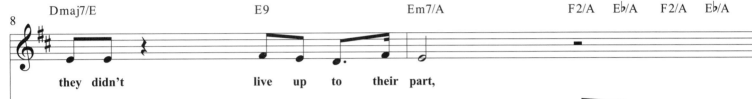

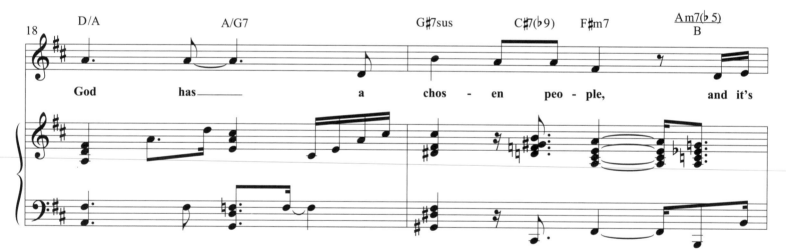

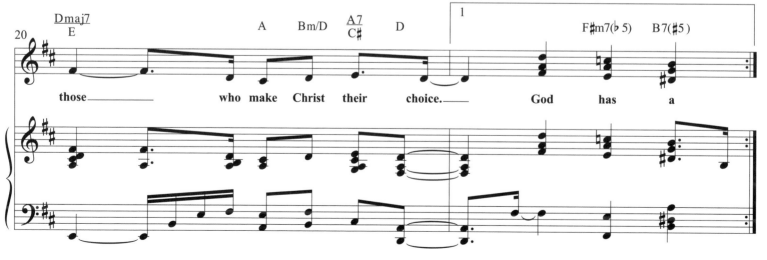

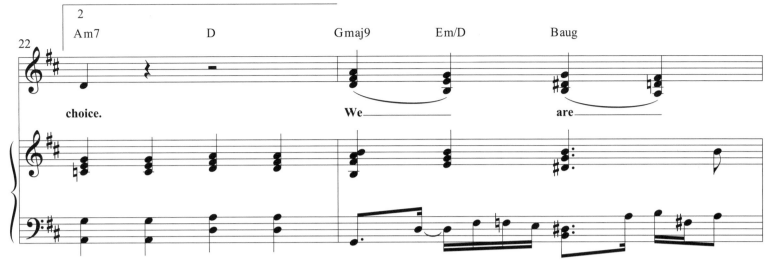

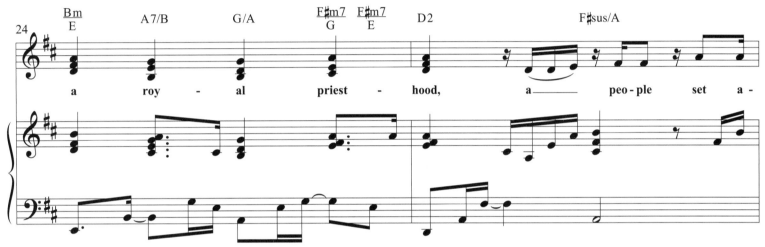

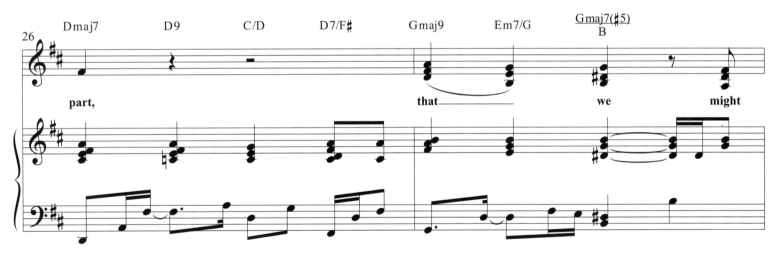

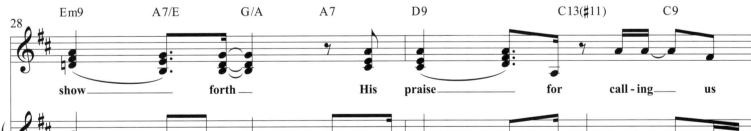

out of the dark. He called us in-to the

mar - vel-ous light, and for this we lift our voice.

God has a

chos - en peo - ple, and it's those who make Christ their choice.

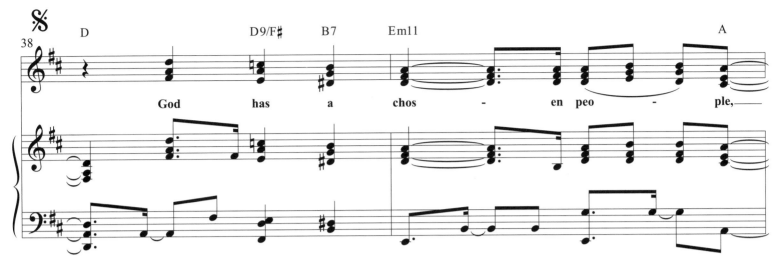

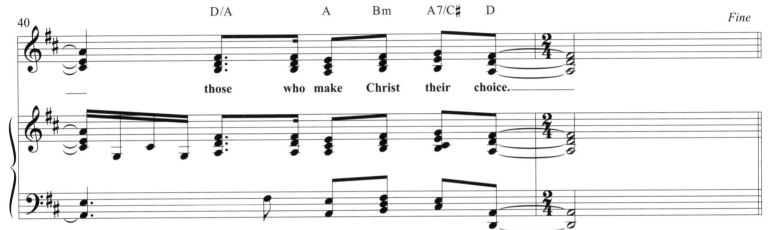

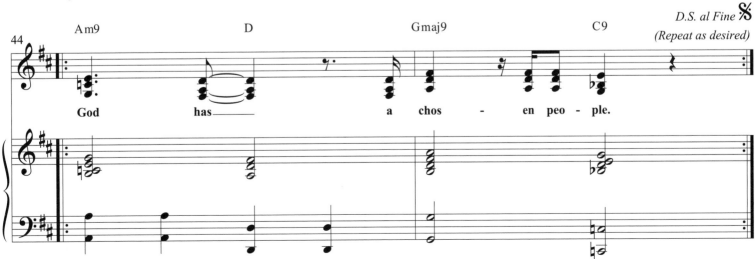

# Your Grace and Mercy

Words and Music by
**FRANKLIN D. WILLIAMS**

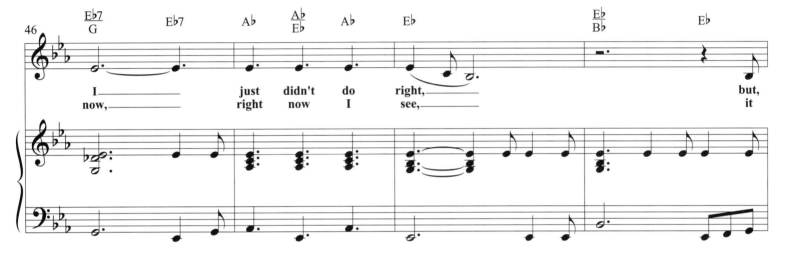

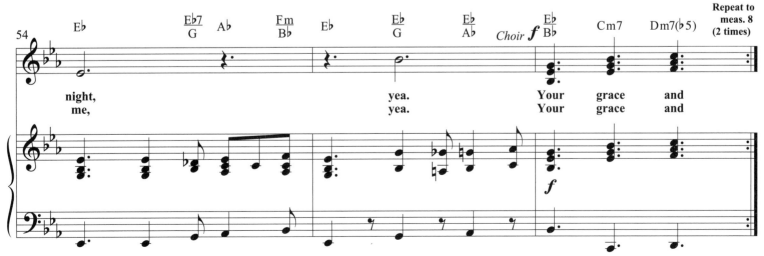

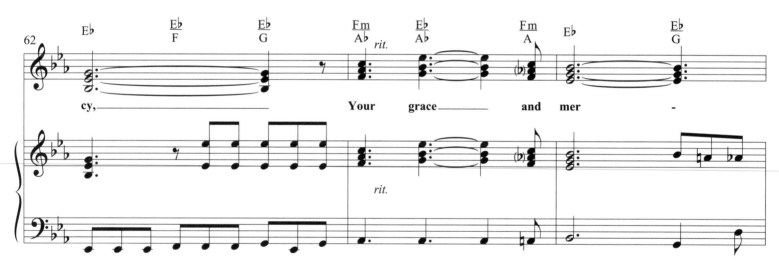

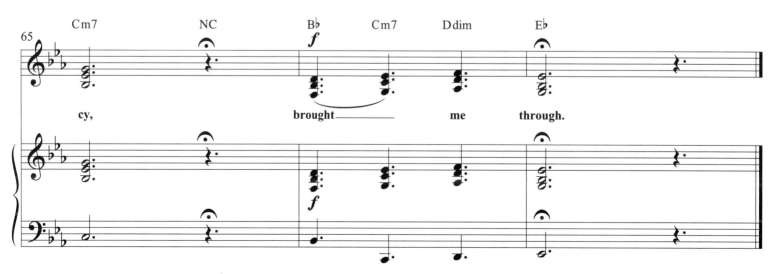

# Saved

Piano Score by
**DON T. THIGPEN**

*Words and Music by*
**DAVID R. CURRY, JR.**

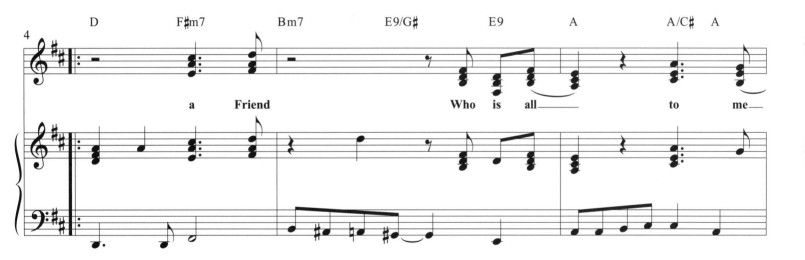

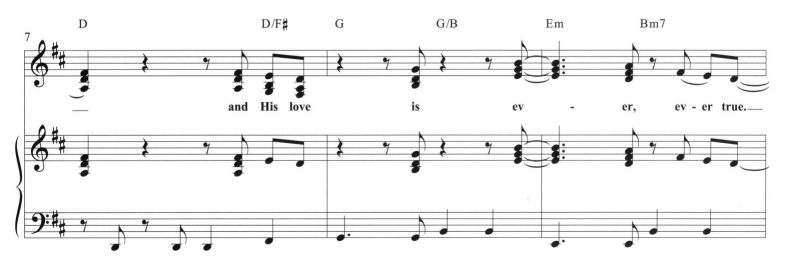

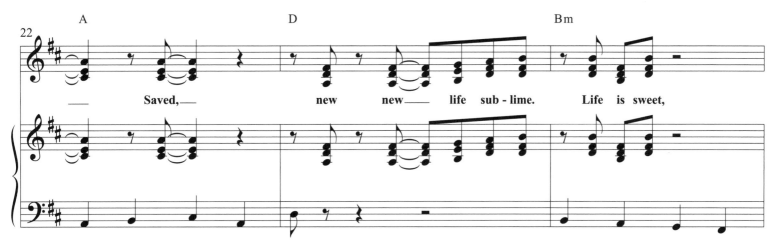

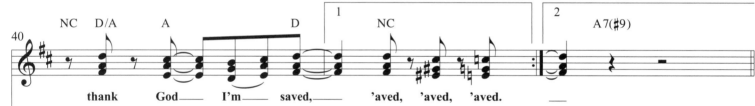

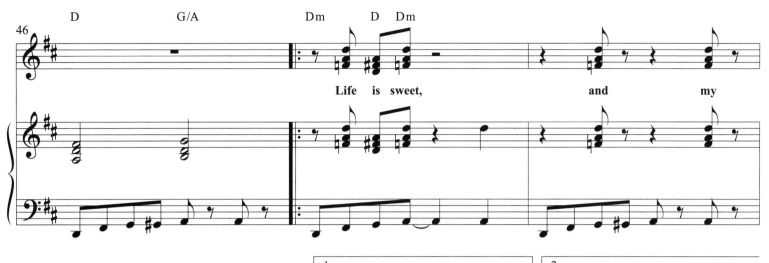

Life is sweet, and my

joy's com-plete.

I'm saved,— I'm saved,— I'm saved,—

I'm saved.— I'm saved,— life is sweet.

# Hold On, Old Soldier

*Piano Score by*
**DON THIGPEN**

*Words and Music by*
**WALTER HAWKINS**

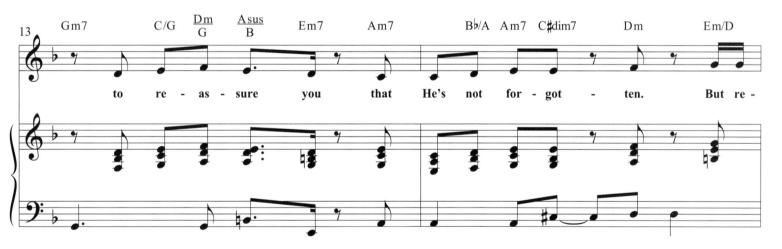

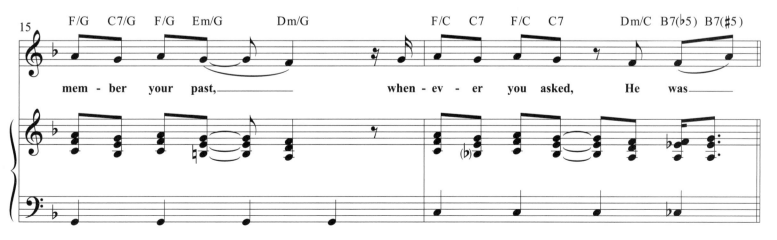

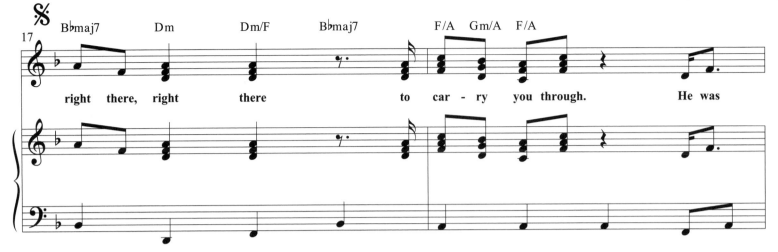

right there, right there to car - ry you through. He was

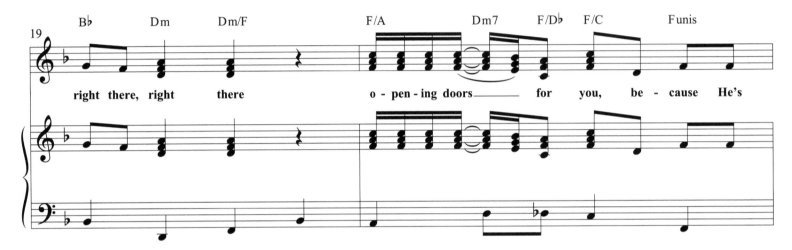

right there, right there o - pen - ing doors for you, be - cause He's

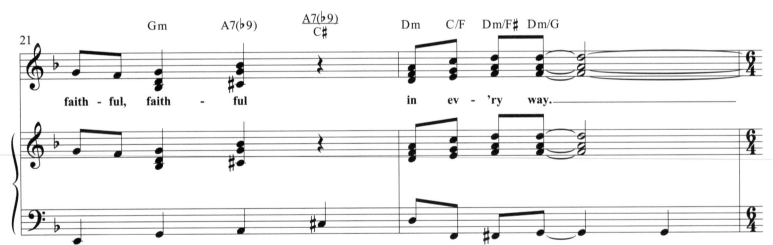

faith - ful, faith - ful in ev - 'ry way.

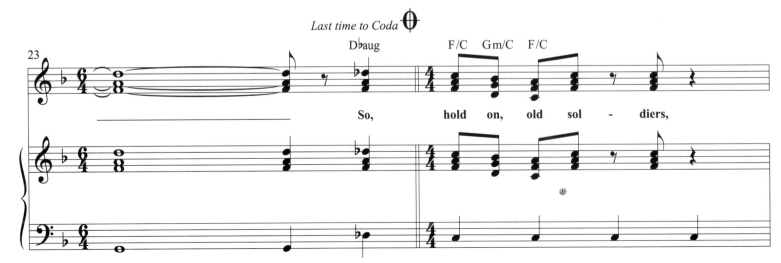

So, hold on, old sol - diers,

don't you ev - er give up. Hold on, old sol - diers,

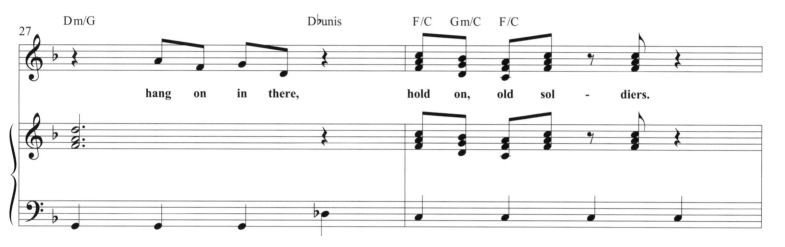

hang on in there, hold on, old sol - diers.

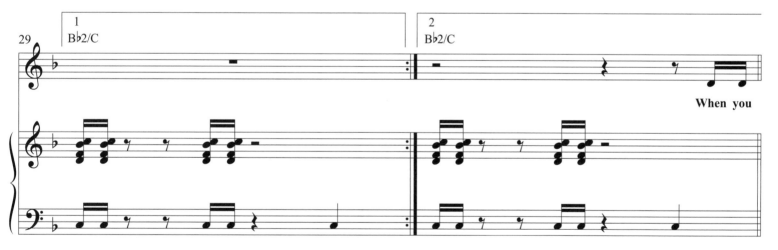

When you

get up off of your knees,— And the world you must face; Re -

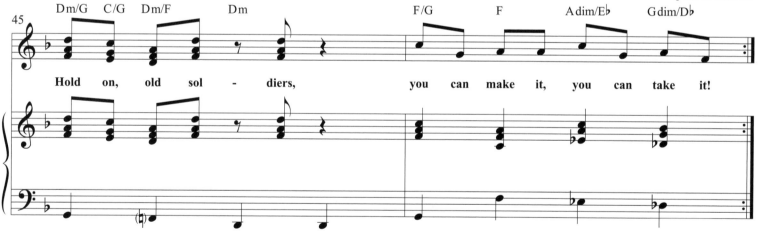

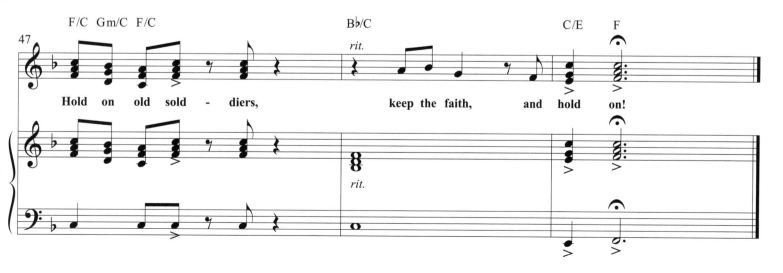

# It's Good to Know Jesus

*Piano Score by*
**DON THIGPEN**

*Words and Music by*
**FRANKLIN D. WILLIAMS**

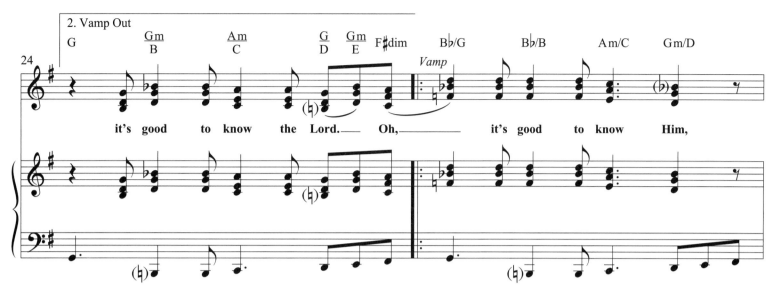

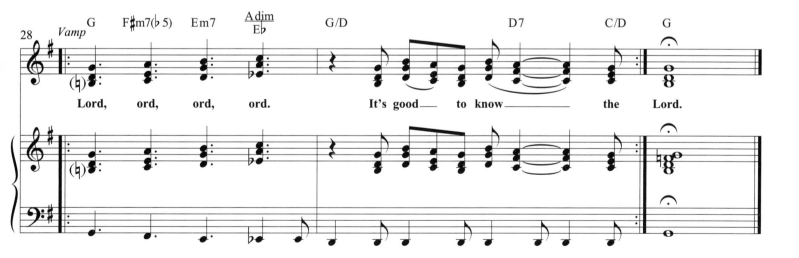

*VERSE 2:*

I love the Lord, He heard m;y cry,
And pitited every groan;
'Long as I live while trouble rise,
I'll hast'n unto His throne.

# I Get Excited

*Piano Score by*
**DON T. THIGPEN**

*Words and Music by*
**DAVID R. CURRY**

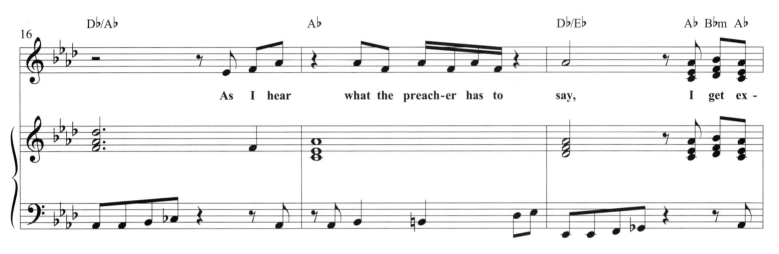

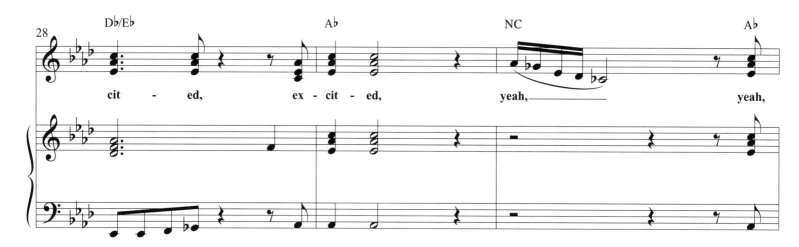

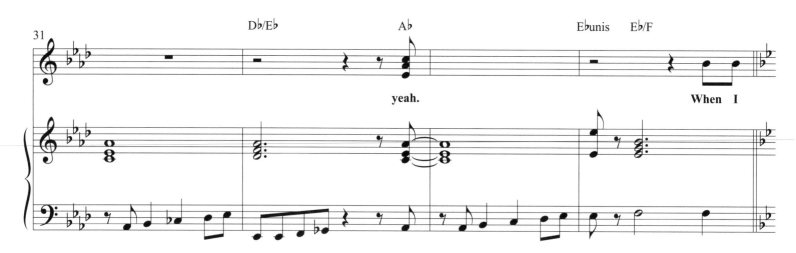

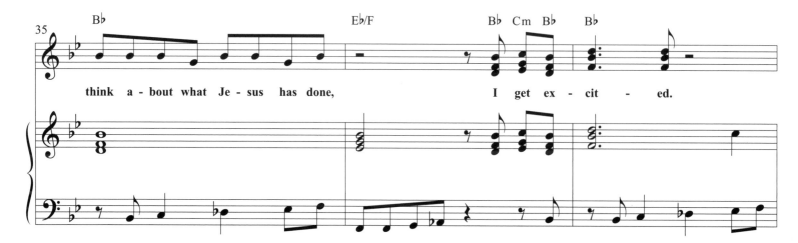

And the choir be - gins to sing their songs, I get ex -

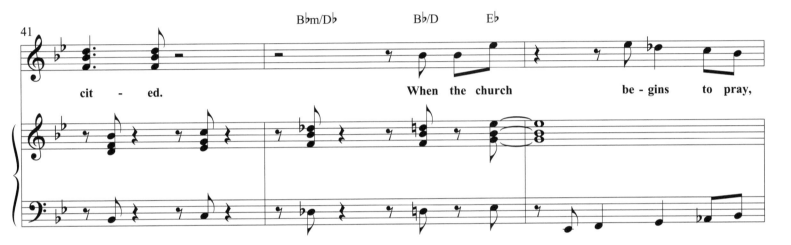

cit - ed. When the church be - gins to pray,

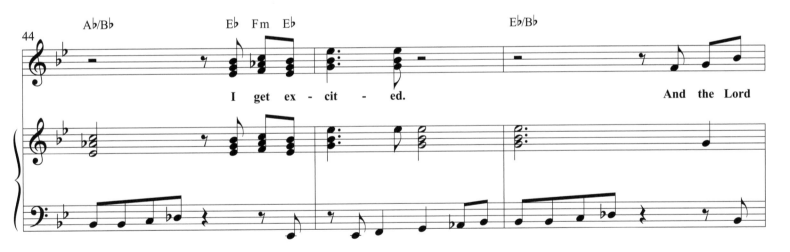

I get ex - cit - ed. And the Lord

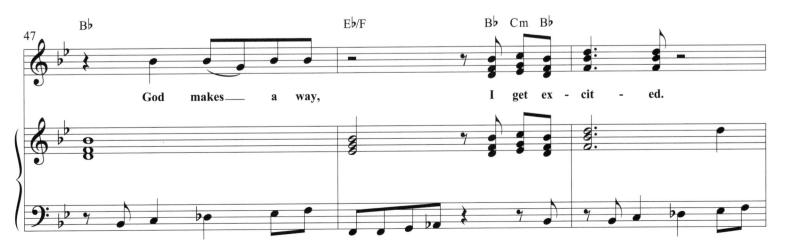

God makes— a way, I get ex - cit - ed.

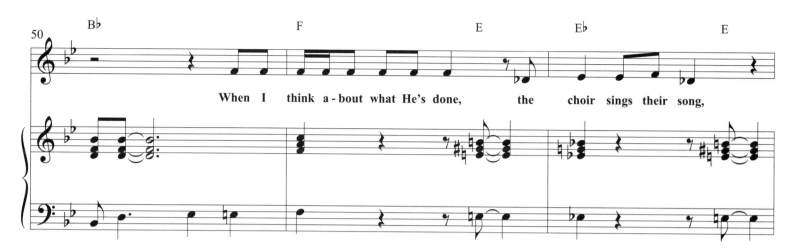

When I think a-bout what He's done, the choir sings their song,

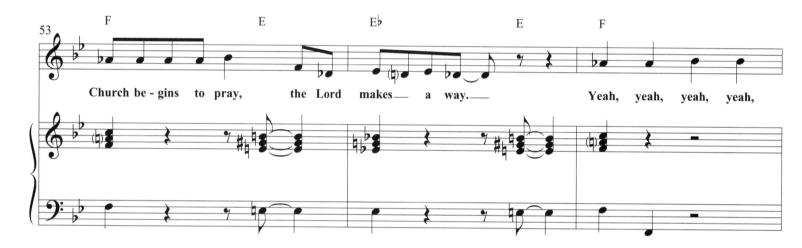

Church be-gins to pray, the Lord makes a way. Yeah, yeah, yeah, yeah,

yeah, yeah. I get ex-cit-ed, ex-cit-ed, ex-

cit-ed, yeah, yeah,

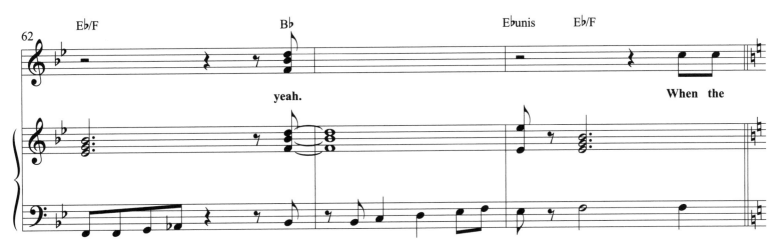

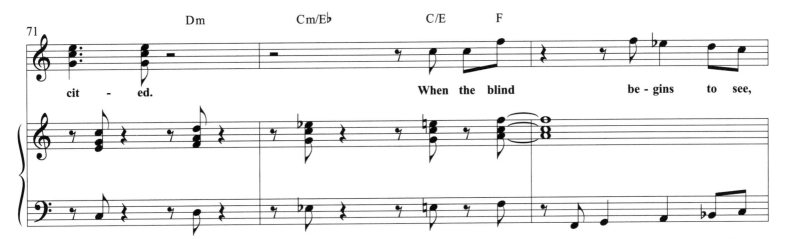

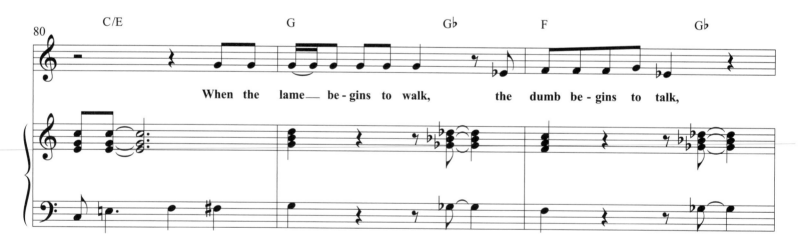

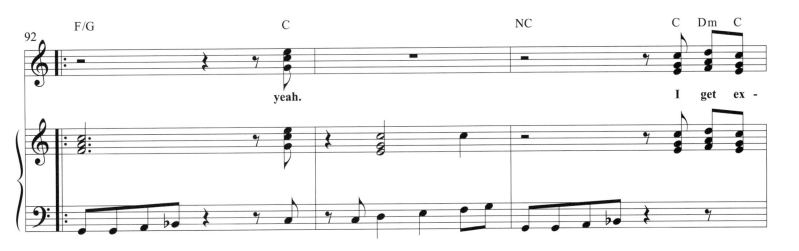

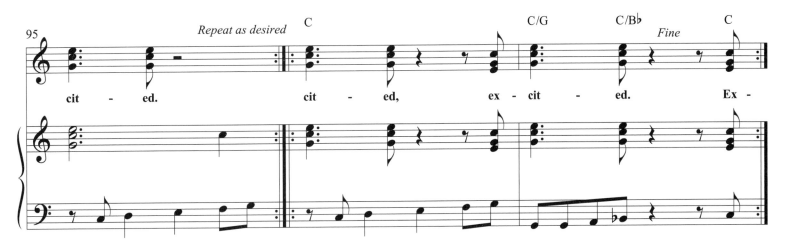

# Near the Cross

*Arranged by*
**DAVID R. CURRY**

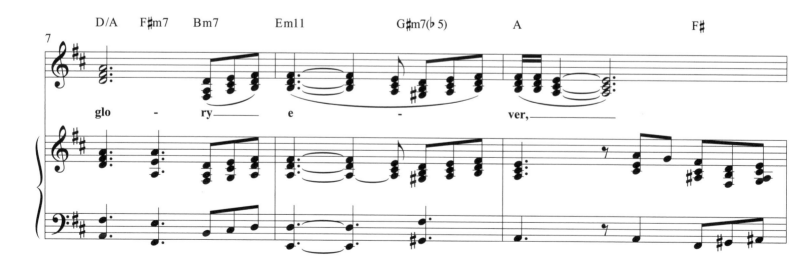

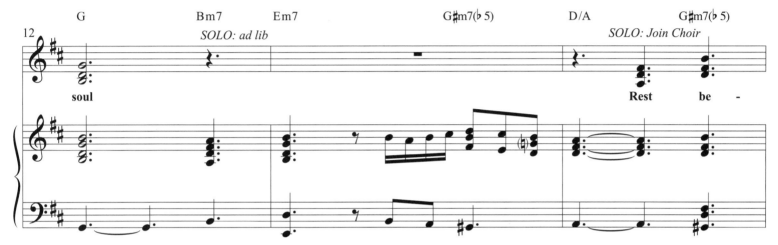

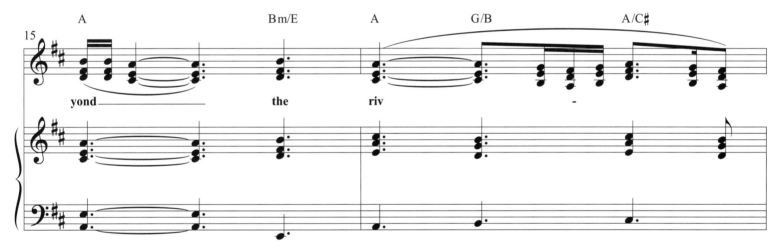

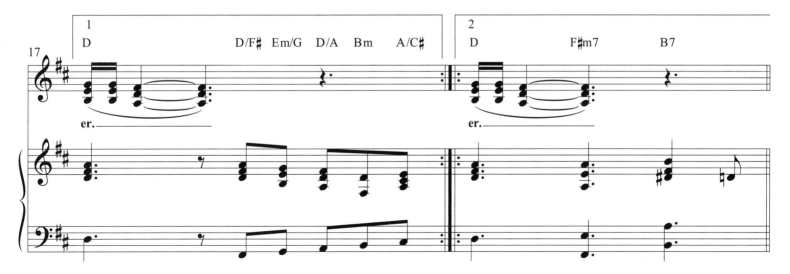

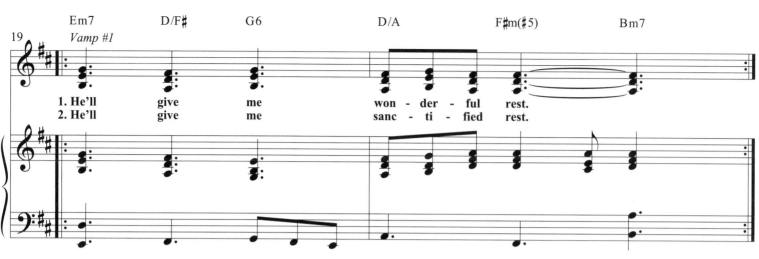

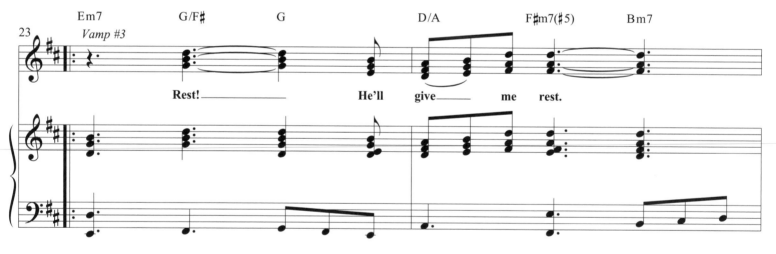

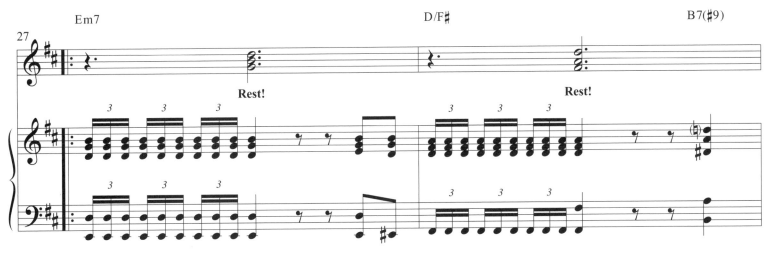

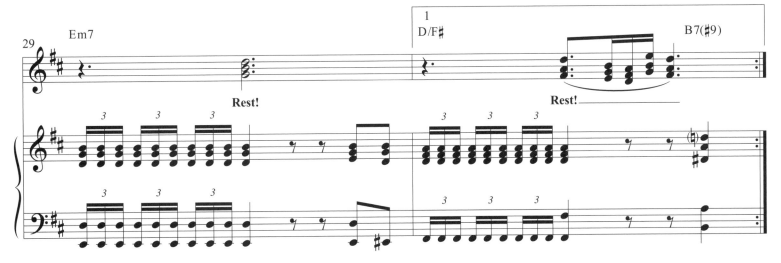

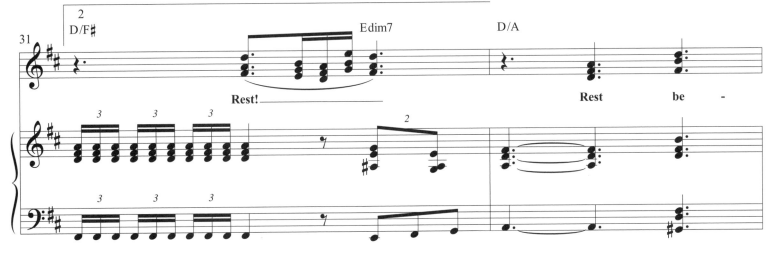

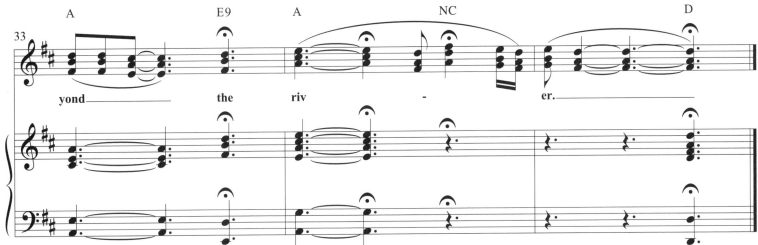

# Thank You for My Mansion

Piano Score by
**DON T. THIGPEN**

*Words and Music by*
**FRANKLIN WILLIAMS**
*and* **JEFFREY LaVALLEY**

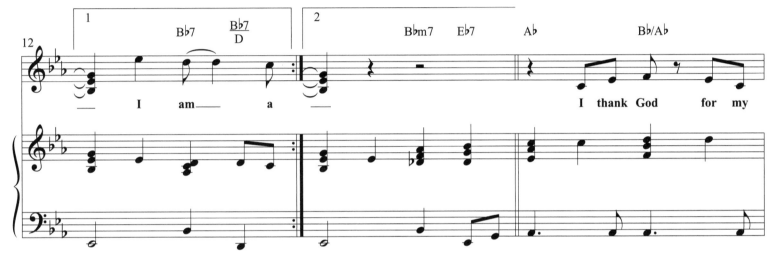

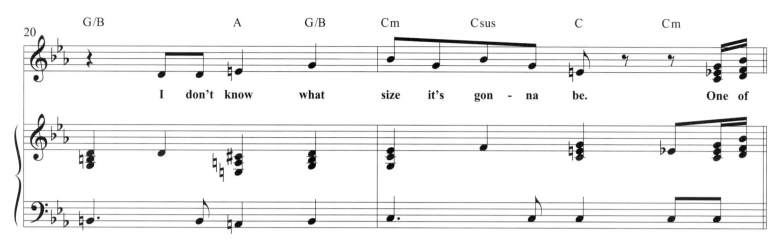

I don't know what size it's gon - na be. One of

them be - longs to me, one of them be - longs to me.

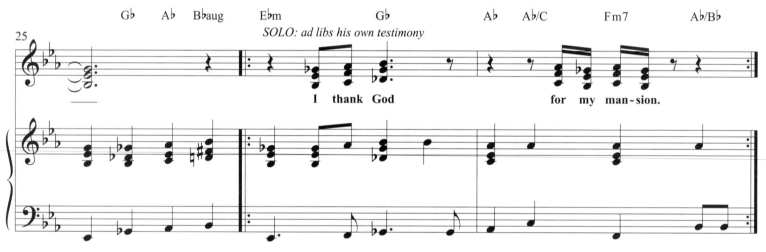

*SOLO: ad libs his own testimony*

I thank God for my man - sion.

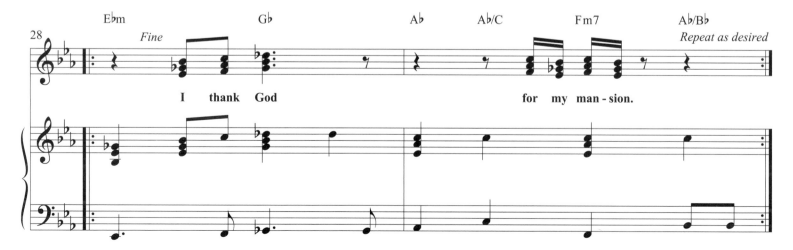

*Fine*

*Repeat as desired*

I thank God for my man - sion.

# He Can Fix What Is Broke

*Words and Music by*
**JAMES MITCHELL**

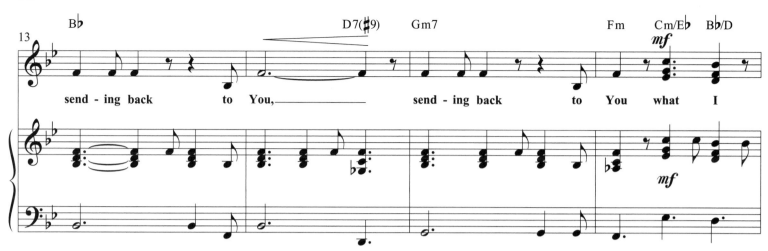

send - ing back to You,_____ send - ing back to You what I

can - not re - pair,_____ I can - not re - pair. So, You can

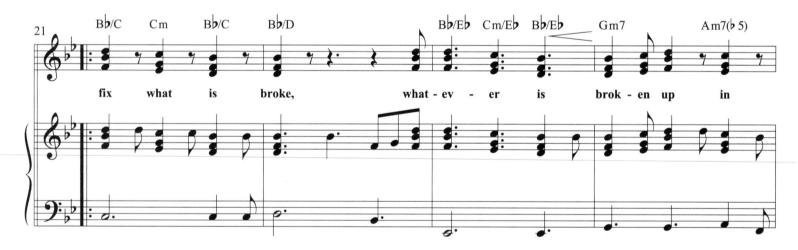

fix what is broke, what - ev - er is brok - en up in

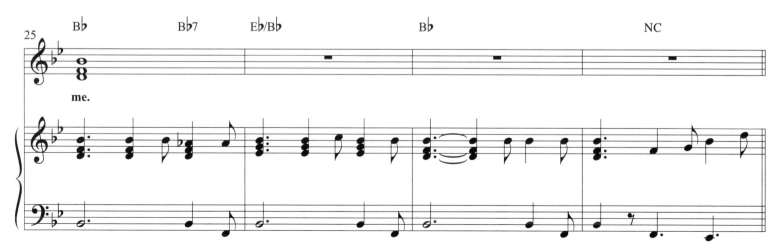

me.

The Fath - er looked and He saw_____ a ves - sel_____

that was torn a - part, He held it in His arms and then He gave it

*2nd time:* He held me in tHIs arms and then He gave me

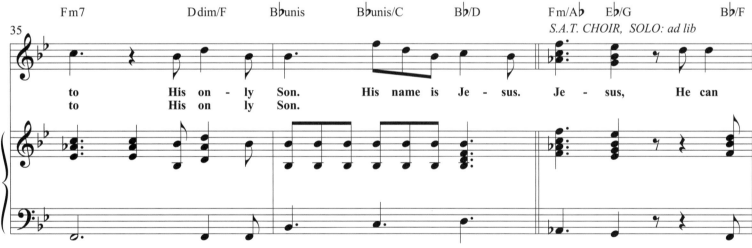

to His on - ly Son. His name is Je - sus. Je - sus, He can

to His on - ly Son.

fix what ev - er is brok - en Je - sus; 'Tell you I gave Him my heart. I

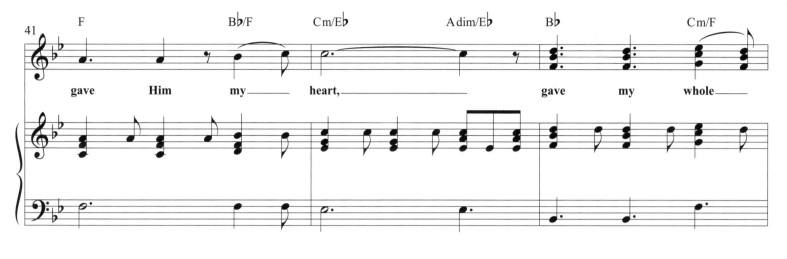

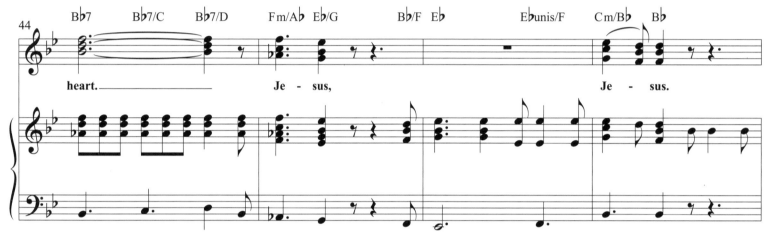

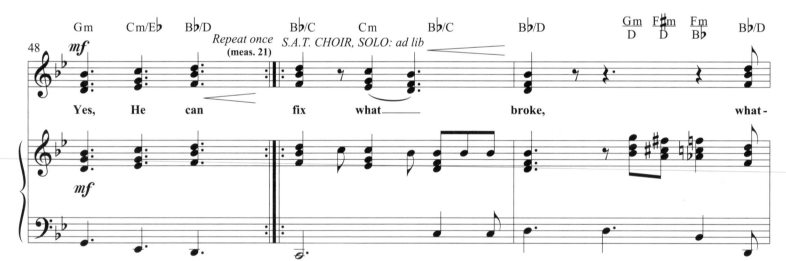

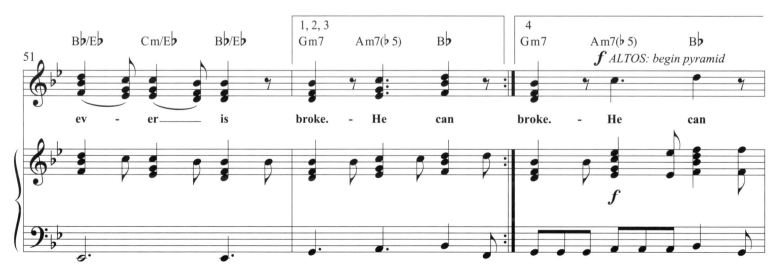

# It Was Worth It All

*Piano Score by*
**DON T. THIGPEN**

*Words and Music by*
**BENJAMIN CONE, JR.**

soul's been___ saved,___ my life's been re - ar-ranged,___

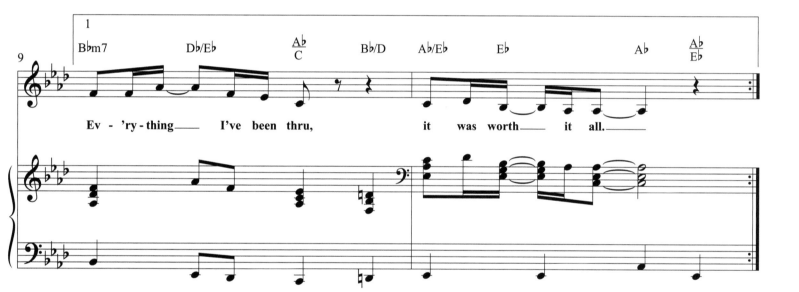

Ev - 'ry-thing___ I've been thru, it was worth___ it all.___

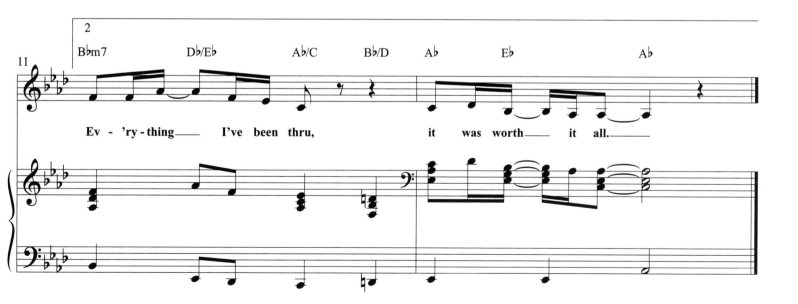

Ev - 'ry-thing___ I've been thru, it was worth___ it all.___

# Jesus Paid It All

*Piano Score by*
**DON T. THIGPEN**

*Words and Music by*
**DAVID R. CURRY**

# EXCITING NEW SONGBOOKS
## from SHAWNEE PRESS

# Check Out Another Great "Play-Along" Product from Shawnee Press!

## Simple Spirituals for Piano

### Fun and Easy-to-play settings

Simple Spirituals for Piano brings together some of the best-loved spirituals of all time in fun and easy-to-play settings. *Bonus:* The book comes with its own CD, which is great for rehearsal, performance or simply personal enjoyment as you play along.

The CD also contains demonstration performances, especially helpful for pianists learning these songs for the first time. These classic songs make this collection a spirit-filled and refreshing addition to your piano library.

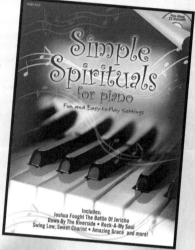

## Songs include:

*Ain't That Good News!*

*Amazing Grace*

*Deep River*

*Do Lord, Remember Me*

*Down By The Riverside*

*Every Time I Feel The Spirit*

*Ezekiel Saw The Wheel*

*Go Down Moses*

*Go, Tell It On The Mountain*

*He's Got The Whole World In His Hands*

*In The Sweet By And By*

*Jesus Loves Me*

*Joshua Fought The Battle Of Jericho*

*Lord, I Want To Be A Christian*

*Peace Like A River*

*Ride On, King Jesus*

*Rock-A-My-Soul*

*Steal Away*

*Swing Low, Sweet Chariot*

*This Little Light Of Mine*

*Wade In The Water*

*Were You There*

## Shawnee Press, Inc.

www.shawneepress.com/songbooks

Available from your favorite music retailer